WEST CHICAGO PUBLIC LIBRARY DISTRICT

3 6653 00140 6218

W9-BSL-313

West Chicago Public Library District
118 West Washington
West Chicago, IL 60185-2803
Phone # (630) 231-1552

FORCES AND GRAVITY

Please visit our web site at: **www.garethstevens.com**
For a free color catalog describing Gareth Stevens Publishing's list of high-quality books and multimedia programs, call 1-800-542-2595 (USA) or 1-800-387-3178 (Canada). Gareth Stevens Publishing's fax: (414) 332-3567.

Library of Congress Cataloging-in-Publication Data

Move.
     Forces and gravity.
       p. cm. — (Discovery Channel school science. Universes large and small)
     Summary: Discusses forces such as air pressure, inertia, and gravity, and how they affect daily life. Includes related activities.
     ISBN 0-8368-3368-6 (lib. bdg.)
     1. Gravity—Juvenile literature. 2. Motion—Juvenile literature. [1. Gravity.
2. Motion. 3. Force and energy.] I. Title. II. Series.
QC178.M68 2003
531'.14—dc21
                                  2003042496

This edition first published in 2004 by
Gareth Stevens Publishing
A World Almanac Education Group Company
330 West Olive Street, Suite 100
Milwaukee, WI 53212 USA

This U.S. edition copyright © 2004 by Gareth Stevens, Inc. First published in 2000 as *Move: The Forces & Gravity Files* by Discovery Enterprises, LLC, Bethesda, Maryland. © 2000 by Discovery Communications, Inc.

Further resources for students and educators available at
www.discoveryschool.com

Designed by Bill SMITH STUDIO
Creative Director: Ron Leighton
Designers: Nick Stone, Sonia Gauba, Bill Wilson, Dmitri Kushnirsky,
    Darren D'Agostino, Joe Bartos
Photo Editors: Jennifer Friel, Scott Haag
Art Buyers: Paula Radding, Marianne Tozzo

Gareth Stevens Editor: Betsy Rasmussen
Gareth Stevens Art Director: Tammy Gruenewald
Technical Advisor: Russell Berg

All rights reserved to Gareth Stevens, Inc. No part of this book may be reproduced, stored in a retrieval system, or transmitted in any form or by any means, electronic, mechanical, photocopying, recording, or otherwise, without the prior written permission of the publisher except for the inclusion of brief quotations in an acknowledged review.

Printed in the United States of America

1 2 3 4 5 6 7 8 9 07 06 05 04 03

Writers: Robin Doak, John-Ryan Hevron, Scott Ingram, Anna Prokos, Rachel Roswal, Denise Vega

Editor: Anna Prokos

Photographs: p. 2, pilot's face, UPI/CORBIS-Bettmann; p. 3, globe, MapArt; p. 3, sky diver, Robbie Culver/Skydreams Productions; pp. 4-5, pilot's face, UPI/CORBIS-Bettmann; p. 9, Shannon Lucid, NASA; p. 9, Wright Brothers, Discover Communications, Inc.; pp. 14-15, Robbie Culver/Skydreams Productions; p. 16, Emmit Smith, Peter Reed Miller/Sports Illustrated; p. 17, Mark McGwire, John E. Biever/Sports Illustrated; pp. 20-21, black hole, © PhotoDisc; p.14, Galileo, © Archive Photos; p. 23, Galileo's experiment, Bettmann/ CORBIS; p. 25, cycler, Digital Stock; p. 26, Rocket, Digital Stock; p. 27, planet, Digital Stock; p. 27, Hand Computer, © Ron Leighton; p. 27, magnifying glass, Digital Stock; p. 28, Newton, © Bill Sanderson/Science Photo Dept./Photo Researchers; p. 29, defying gravity, NASA; Cover and all other photography, © COREL.

Illustrations: p. 18-19, spook or science, Ron Tanovitz.

Acknowledgements: p. 14-15, eyewitness story, Carl P.E. dos Santos, http://www.adventureliving.com; p. 28, excerpts from MEMOIRS OF SIR ISSAC NEWTON'S LIFE. © 1936 by William Stuckeley. Reprinted by permission of Taylor & Francis; p. 29, excerpts from DO YOUR EARS POP IN SPACE? © 1997 by R. Mike Mullane. Reprinted by permission of John Wiley & Sons.

What's up with forces and gravity? Lots. Without gravity, you'd be floating around your classroom right now. And without the forces that work with gravity, you'd have a hard time completing everyday tasks, such as walking up the stairs to get to class. Everything and everyone depends on forces and gravity to function. And we have famous scientists such as Sir Isaac Newton and Galileo Galilei to thank for explaining how these forces work together in nature—and how you're affected by them.

In FORCES AND GRAVITY, you'll embark on a journey to black holes, tightropes, the Leaning Tower of Pisa, and dozens of other places that will help you make sense of forces and gravity. Plus, Discovery Channel will tell you about the science behind some famous football players and how stacking up a bunch of cookies shows an object's center of gravity. So get ready to get down with forces and gravity.

FORCES AND GRAVITY

Simply air-resistible. See page 14

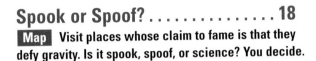

Forces & Gravity

H ave you ever been on a roller coaster or a spinning carnival ride? You probably remember what if felt like: your stomach churned as you lifted up from your seat when you raced down a steep hill or around a sharp loop. And if you've been on an elevator that suddenly rose or dropped quickly, your stomach probably did a slight flip-flop. The feelings you got from those experiences were caused by forces and gravity. And extreme forces, like this man is being subjected to, have noticeable effects on your body.

Such extreme forces are unusual in everyday life. Mostly, we don't even notice the forces that affect us. Gravity pulls us down toward the center of Earth, but that's not a force you feel. As Earth spins, you travel along with it at an amazing speed, and you don't feel that either. Air pressure weighs down on you all the time without your even noticing it. Forces affect you all the time, but are such a normal part of daily life

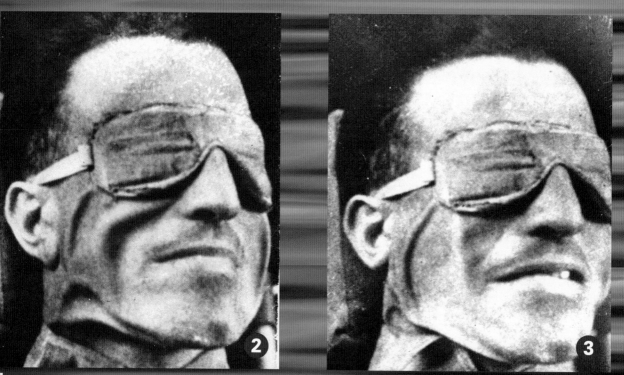

that it takes a whole lot of force to make you aware of how strong they can really be.

But there's no need to tell the person in these pictures how strong forces can be. He can feel it. He's a pilot, undergoing experiments in a wind tunnel and being subjected to increasing G forces (as shown in each panel). G stands for gravity, and a G force is the force of gravity on an object on Earth. Twice that force is 2 G, three times that force is 3 G, and so on. The more G forces a person is subjected to, the more pressure that is exerted on his or her body. Which is what's causing this man's face to be lifted up and back. The stronger the G force, the more his face is affected. Luckily, you aren't subjected to extremely strong G forces everyday—or you'd be walking around looking like this man.

Though it may not look like it, he's even affected by a property related to force in panel one. It's the same property you're subjected to right now: inertia. Sir Isaac Newton described inertia as the property by which an object at rest tends to stay at rest until a force acts upon it. And an object in motion tends to stay in motion until an outside force acts upon it, which is what is beginning to happen in panel two— a stronger G force is acting upon him, causing his skin to be pulled tight against his bones.

When you take a ride on a roller coaster or other amusement park ride, you're subjected to more than 1 G, but usually not more than 3 G. At 3.5 G, a person may suffer a nose bleed. At 4 G, a person feels extreme, almost unbearable, pressure. At 6 G, a person may become unconscious. Amusement park ride engineers make sure that their ride doesn't exceed the limits—so you can be physically thrilled as you ride again and again.

Astronauts who are training for space aren't always comfortable. They're put through really strong G force experiments so their bodies can be prepared for when they blast through and out of Earth's atmosphere. Like the man in these panels, they're subjected to more than 3 G forces. And when they finally exit Earth's atmosphere, they're subjected to zero gravity—quite a difference from multiple G forces.

Here, you'll read all about these forces. You'll learn which forces are the strongest and which are real weaklings. You'll go into the minds of the scientists who first studied these forces, and find out who the people are who are most affected by forces and gravity today. But you'll do all of this at a comfortable 1 G. So sit back, relax, and may the forces be with you.

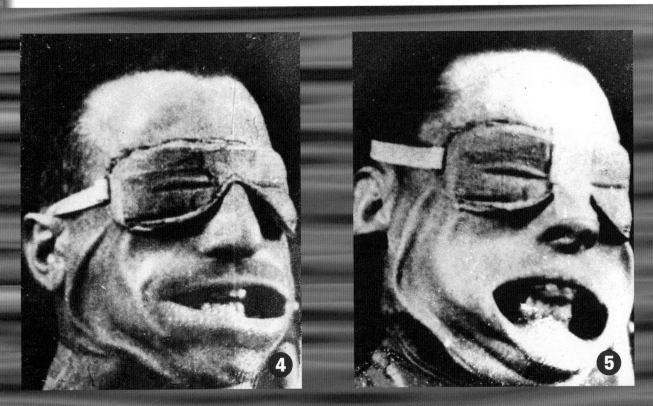

Down With Gravity

Q: So, you're the apple that hit Newton on his head?

A: Yup. That's me, the real McCoy.

Q: What? The real Macintosh?

A: No. The real McCoy. I'm the real thing. The apple that hit Sir Isaac Newton over the head—sort of. I was aiming for his head. Not to hurt the man, of course—I'm not a rotten apple. I just wanted to knock some gravity into him. But I missed—and hit the ground next to him instead.

Q: So did you get your point across?

A: You bet. The sound I made when I hit the ground got Newton thinking.

Q: Thinking about what?

A: Gravity, of course! And the Moon.

Q: The Moon?

A: Yes, the Moon. Newton was a pretty far-out guy. When he saw me hit the ground, he thought, 'the power that brought the apple from the tree to the ground must not be limited to the surface of Earth. Why should that apple always descend perpendicularly to the ground? Why should it not go sideways or upward, but constantly to Earth's center?'

Q: Meaning?

A: Meaning that this power must also reach out beyond Earth—like to the Moon. That since I'm above the ground, and so is the Moon, then Earth's gravity should affect the Moon as well as the apple. A friend of Izzy's—that's my pet name for Isaac Newton— heard him say about gravity,

'Why not as high as the Moon? If so, that must influence her motion and perhaps retain her in her orbit.'

Q: Her who?

A: Her, the Moon.

Q: But the Moon doesn't hit Earth like you hit the ground.

A: Right. That's what Newton realized. When I fell from the tree to the ground, he saw that my velocity accelerated as I moved toward the ground. Then he thought that there must be a force that acted on me to cause me to speed up as I fell. That Izzy, he was one smart guy.

Q: So what did he think that force was?

A: Gravity—with a capital G. He realized that things falling toward the ground went faster because gravity was pulling them down. And he realized that no matter how tall the apple tree was, I'd still fall to the ground. Then, he got to the core of the matter.

Q: Which was?

A: Which was that the orbit of the Moon could be affected by the gravitational force of Earth. Because acceleration due to gravity could change the velocity of the Moon so that it followed an orbit around Earth.

Q: Can you pare that down, Apple?

A: Sorry. I got carried away. Well, I don't ever really get carried away—you know, because of gravity. And that's why the Moon doesn't go flying off too. Well, gravity in combination with something else. See, the Moon's motion can be thought of as two kinds of motion working together. Gravity causes the Moon to move directly down to the center of Earth, but another part of the Moon's motion is at right angles to the first, or sideways to Earth. The two together result in a nearly circular orbit.

Q: Did you always know all this about motion and gravity?

A: Of course. My relatives have been falling off our family tree for ages. But I was the smart one who made someone take notice.

Q: So you're saying you should be given credit for "discovering" gravity?

A: You didn't hear those words come out of my core. But I'm not going to argue with you. Mr. Newton had the brains, but I had the vision. Can you imagine how history would have been different if I didn't take a fall near Izzy? I mean, give credit where credit is due.

Q: What would have happened if you didn't fall near Newton? Don't you think something else would have caused someone to think about gravity?

A: Who knows? Maybe the force of gravity would never have been realized, and Izzy would have gone about living an ordinary life. And people all over the world wouldn't know about this story. And apples wouldn't be given the respect and credit they deserve.

Q: You mean gravity would not be given the respect it deserves?

A: Gravity, too—I guess. Without gravity, I would have just floated around. I broke free from the tree branch.

Q: Like astronauts float around in space?

A: You could say so. But you'll have to ask my Granny about that. My Granny Smith. She's the expert on space. Me? I'm just the one with the juicy details about gravity.

Activity

MOON MADNESS Earth has only one Moon, and when it comes to gravity, the two work as a team. Earth's gravity holds the Moon in orbit, and the Moon causes the oceans' tides. But what is the gravitational relationship between other planets and their moons? Get together with some classmates. Each person should pick one planet and thoroughly research it and its moons, noting number of moons, sizes of planets and moons, and distances apart. Then put everyone's information together and try to see patterns and draw conclusions.

Ups and Downs

How do we know so much about the powerful force that pulls objects down toward Earth? We can thank curious people who spent a lot of time looking up at the stars, planets, and moons. In time, they learned all about this invisible "glue" that holds us all together. And in even more time, they successfully defied it. Nothing can really hold science down—not even gravity.

Copernicus

8¢US

16th Century

1514: Nicolaus Copernicus, a Polish scientist, writes *On the Revolutions of the Celestial Spheres*, a book in which he points out that all of the planets, including Earth, revolve around the Sun. This is against the belief at the time that the Sun revolves around Earth—the theory of geocentricity. He paves the way for future break-throughs by Galileo, Newton, and others.

1592: Astronomer Galileo Galilei adds to the under-standing of gravity with experiments showing that falling bodies of different weights fall at the same rate. In the next century, he is threatened with death for supporting Copernicus's belief that Earth orbits the Sun.

17th Century

1609: Johannes Kepler shows that the planets move in oval-shaped orbits, but he thinks they are kept in place by some kind of invisible structure.

1687: Among other revolutionary findings, Isaac Newton shows that a force attracting planets toward the Sun is also what keeps them orbiting around it. He extends this theory to include comets.

18th Century

1705: Edward Halley uses Newton's ideas on comets' orbits around the Sun to predict the return in 1758 of a comet previously seen in 1531, 1607, and 1682. The comet showed up on schedule and became known as Halley's comet. (Halley had paid for the publication of Newton's book, *Principia*.)

1782: The Montgolfier brothers invent the air balloon, a significant step in getting air travel "off the ground"—and breaking gravity's Earthly hold.

19th Century

1890s: German aeronautical engineer Otto Lilienthal conducts important experiments with glider flights. These experiments are of major help to others in the field of aerodynamics, including the Wright Brothers.

20th Century

1903: On December 17, Wilbur and Orville Wright become the first people to feel the effects of defying gravity by flying in a power-controlled aircraft near Kitty Hawk, North Carolina. Each brother makes two trips, but Wilbur's trip is the longest, lasting about 59 seconds. The distance covered? About 853 feet (260 meters). Today's 747s require 10,000 feet (3048 m) just to take off.

1969: On July 20, American astronauts Neil Armstrong and Edwin "Buzz" Aldrin become the first humans to walk on the Moon, where gravity is one-sixth that of Earth's gravitational pull. As he takes his first step onto the surface, Armstrong states, "That's one small step for man, one giant leap for mankind."

1990s: NASA's *KC-135* aircraft is used to film weightless scenes for the movie *Apollo 13*, based on the real mission. Scientists use the atmosphere of "microgravity" to learn about how various fluids react in an environment with little or no gravity. Also called the "Vomit Comet," this aircraft is used to test the effects of flying in zero gravity. Based on the maneuvers it performs, passengers on the turbo jet experience short periods of what feels like weightlessness, often resulting in motion sickness. The queasiness subsides after a couple of flights.

1996: Astronaut Shannon Lucid is the first American to spend 188 consecutive days on the Russian Space Station Mir, joining Russian cosmonauts Yuri Usachev and Yuri Onufriyenko. While traveling through space, the trio followed a regulated exercise schedule to keep their muscles from weakening in the weightless atmosphere of the aircraft. Lucid conducted an experiment that showed that plants, as well as oxygen, can be produced in microgravity.

10¢ AIR MAIL
UNITED STATES
FIRST MAN ON THE MOON

Shannon Lucid

9

SPEED

On the Air!

If you dropped a feather and a bowling ball off your roof, which would hit the ground first? Easy, the bowling ball! But if your house were in a vacuum—a place without any air—the same feather and bowling ball would hit the ground at the same time. Why? Because acceleration due to gravity is the same, regardless of the object's mass. That's why a heavy object and a light object fall at the same rate in a vacuum. Also, in a vacuum, there aren't any air molecules to slow the objects down. Outside of a vacuum, an object's surface area will encounter more friction from air molecules—air resistance—which will in turn slow it down. Also, outside a vacuum, an object changes its speed at a different rate due to wind resistance.

This principle is also true for skydivers. Though the speed at which skydivers plummet toward Earth depends somewhat on their weight in relation to how quickly the air molecules slow them down, it also depends on how they hold their bodies. If skydivers straighten out their bodies and shoot down head or feet first, they'll slice through the air with very little resistance. However, if they float facedown with arms and legs spread out, the larger surface area will create more wind resistance because of the friction of air molecules. That will make them float down slower. When they open their parachutes, the greater surface area of the parachutes create even more air resistance and slows them down so they don't crash.

RACERS

Glued to the Track

Racing cars are designed to cut through the air. Maybe that's why they have so much in common with the wing of a plane. At high speeds, Indy race cars can be very unstable. To compensate for this, racing cars utilize the same concept as the plane wing, though for an opposite reaction. Car designs use the wind to provide a downward force to glue the car to the track. The car's body is similar to an upside-down airplane wing. The air moving under the car moves faster than the air above it, which pushes the car onto the track. Cars sometimes even use small wings in the front and rear to generate more downward force.

It's a Bird, It's a Plane

The aerodynamics involved in birds' wings and in airplanes are very similar. Basically, both use wings to take advantage of the Bernoulli Principle: Air pressure decreases as air speed increases. Air moves faster over the upper, curved surface of an airplane or bird wing than it does over the flatter lower surface. The greater pressure of the slow-moving air pushes the wing up, and lifts it. Both birds and planes have similarly shaped wings; however, they use different methods of propulsion. Birds actually flap their wings downward and backward. That motion pushes air downward and to the rear, creating a lift and forward thrust. On a plane, instead of moving the wings, a powerful engine pushes the wings directly through the air with enough force to cause a lift powerful enough to put the plane in the air.

Activity

HAND IT TO BERNOULLI Hold a sheet of paper in front of you, close to your mouth. Curve the top of it slightly toward you, letting the other end hang down. Now blow hard across the top. What happens? Think of what happens when you stick your hand out of a moving car (but not too far!) with your palm down. What do you feel? In which direction does your hand move? Write a paragraph describing how the paper, your hand, and a bird's wing demonstrate Bernoulli's Principle.

Forces to Be Reckoned With

May the Force Be With You

A force is a push or a pull that causes an object to move. Without force, there would be no motion. Some forces are obvious. When you push a shopping cart, for example, you are using force to propel it forward. There are other forces that you may not be able to see, but they're there just the same. Check out the following:

Gravity: Thanks to gravity, what goes up almost always comes down. Gravity is the force of attraction between objects. All objects exert gravitational force, but the larger an object, the stronger its gravitational pull. Earth's gravity pulls us toward its surface. Our planet's gravitational pull is so strong that it holds the Moon in orbit.

Friction: Is something rubbing you the wrong way? It might be friction—a force that slows an object down. Friction occurs where two objects come in contact with one another. When you drag your feet to slow yourself on a swing, you're using friction. Air resistance is a type of friction. Parachutists experience the opposite forces of gravity and air resistance as they float to the ground.

Inertia: Have you ever been riding in a car when the driver suddenly slams on the brakes? Because of the property of inertia, your body jerks forward. Inertia is not a force but is linked with forces. It is the tendency of an object to continue doing what it is doing until an outside force acts upon it. So your body will keep traveling at the same speed as the car until an outside force stops it. That force could be a safety belt—or a windshield.

Electricity: Electricity is a natural force that is present all around us. Without electrical force, life as we know it would just fall apart. That's because electricity, along with magnetism, helps bind the atoms of all matter together. Static electricity is an electrical force that can cause your clothes to stick together and your hair to stand on end.

Magnetism: Magnetism is a natural force that attracts two objects with different poles, north and south. Magnetism is stronger when two objects with different poles are closer together. The further the objects, the weaker the magnetic force. Did you know that Earth itself is one giant magnet?

Electromagnetic Force: Electrical and magnetic forces work so closely together that they're usually studied as one force, called the electromagnetic force. As an example of how powerful this force is, consider that there are electromagnets strong enough to pick up a car.

Super Forceful! Motion is the result of a force. The greater the force, the greater the motion. Check out these force-full milestones.

- To blast into orbit, the space shuttle needs an engine powerful enough to break gravity's hold. It reaches speeds of up to 17,500 miles (28,158 km) per hour. That's 5 miles (8 km) per second!

- At the 1996 Summer Olympics, Canada's Donavan Bailey was clocked running at 29 miles (47 km) per hour.

- In 1997, Andy Green broke the land-speed record in the *Thrust SCC*. This super-speedy car reached 763 miles (1,228 km) per hour, breaking the sound barrier in the process.

- The fastest jet plane in the world is the United States' SR 71-A. Also known as the *Black Bird,* the plane can travel at speeds of more than 2,400 miles (3,862 km) per hour.

Sir Isaac Newton: Scientific Heavy Hitter

Called the father of modern science, Sir Isaac Newton (1642–1727) was really the first person to understand the concepts of force, motion, and gravity. Newton's theory of universal gravitation states that all objects are attracted to one another. His three laws of motion explain the relationship between gravity, mass, and the distance between two objects.

A Weighty Matter Sometimes you'll hear people talking about mass and weight. What's the difference?

- Mass is the amount of matter in any given object. As long as the object isn't physically changed, its mass always stays the same.

- Weight is a measurement of the force placed on an object by gravity. Scales measure weight. The spring inside a bathroom scale is compressed by the force of a person's weight. The heavier the person, the more the spring is squeezed.

Weight: Lost in Space

Space shuttle astronauts know what it's like to live without gravity. As the shuttle orbits Earth, the combination of gravity and speed of travel creates zero gravity, or weightlessness. With gravity counterbalanced, astronauts hover in space. To get around, they must push and pull themselves from place to place. They even have to strap themselves in while sleeping so they don't hover around the shuttle.

The lack of gravity can have some physical side effects. Shuttle astronauts grow 2 or 3 inches in space as their spines stretch out. That's because there is no gravity to compress their back bones. This condition reverses itself once the astronauts are back on Earth. Other side effects of weightlessness include excess fluids in the face and hands and weakened muscles and bones. These side effects are one reason most shuttle missions don't last for more than two weeks.

Pounds and Planets

The mass of an object does not change with location. The weight of an object does. Because gravity is different on every planet—and on the Sun and Moon—a 100-pound Earth person would weigh the following in other parts of the Solar System. Why would someone weigh more in one space place than another?

SUN, MOON, PLANETS	GRAVITY FACTOR	WEIGHT IN POUNDS*
Sun	27.900	2,790 pounds
Mercury	.284	28 pounds
Venus	.907	91 pounds
Earth	1.000	100 pounds
Earth's Moon	.167	17 pounds
Mars	.380	38 pounds
Jupiter	2.340	234 pounds
Saturn	.925	93 pounds
Uranus	.795	80 pounds
Neptune	1.125	113 pounds
Pluto	.0411	4 pounds

*Rounded

Look Out Below!

A few years ago, Carl P. E. dos Santos fell for skydiving. Today, Carl takes to the skies to test his diving skills—and gravity's force. Here, Carl gives us an account of what it's like to free fall at 120 miles (193 km) an hour, 12,000 feet (3,658 m) above the ground.

Standing in the doorway of the plane you still feel grounded. The equipment weighs heavily on your back, the floor presses against your feet, and the straps pull on your legs and shoulders. Longing for the freedom of flight, you leap. Ten seconds after leaving the plane the wind supports you, fighting against gravity, holding you at a constant speed. Touching nothing but air, you feel the exhilarating rush of adrenaline as you soar through the sky at 120 miles per hour. You are in control; with the slightest movements of your body you alter heading, speed, and position. You and the invisible element seem perfectly in tune, yet the thrill of danger sharpens your focus, slows time, and heightens your senses. Your every nerve tingles with excitement. That smooth collage of color miles below may be where you live, but this is where you are most alive! For sixty seconds of eternity you are completely free of all worldly concerns; it is just you and the sky.

With only one mile left to fall the land has started moving toward you. You now have a glimmer of the immense speed at which you are traveling. As you fall below four thousand feet the earth begins to quickly expand, rushing to meet you. Five short seconds later, a scant three thousand feet left, you open that life-saving piece of cloth. The mad rush of wind suddenly transforms into the peaceful calm of a parachute ride. Slowly your ears adjust to the new volume and you hear the flapping of that beautiful fabric above your head. Eventually gravity reasserts itself; you are now below two hundred feet and the earth is charging up, ready to swallow you. At a mere twelve feet, with a pull on the toggles, you slow your descent and gently set your feet on the ground. You have dared to defy gravity and again you have emerged victorious.

Terminal Velocity

What's happening to dos Santos from a science standpoint? When he takes the plunge, forces and gravity take over. When a diver jumps out of the airplane, he or she moves sideways and down. That creates a floating feeling. Even as the

gravity take over. When a diver jumps out of the airplane, he or she moves sideways and down. That creates a floating feeling. Even as the diver floats, his or her vertical speed increases. After about 10 seconds, air resistance starts pushing up on the diver. Gravity pulls down on the diver at the same time. When the force of air resistance is as strong as the force of gravity, the diver reaches a maximum speed, or terminal velocity. Terminal velocity is the speed at which a diver can fall.

Terminal velocity varies for divers, depending on how they fall. Divers who fall head or feet first can reach more than 180 miles (290 km) an hour. Divers who hold their bodies parallel to the ground as they fall go slower. That's because a horizontal body has more surface area than a body traveling vertically. The larger the surface area, the slower the fall because of air resistance.

Many skydivers fall in a group called a formation. These divers have to slow their fall rate so they can perform tricks and arrange themselves into group formations. Every formation diver holds his or her body parallel to the ground at the same angle so that the entire group falls at the same rate.

How do skydivers slow down enough so that they don't smack into the ground? They use a parachute. At about 2000 feet (610 m) above the ground, the diver pulls on a cord that releases the chute. Once the parachute is opened, the chute's larger area helps air resistance compete with the force of gravity and slows down the diver's fall quickly. Within seconds after opening the parachute, the diver goes from terminal velocity to about 10 miles (16 km) per hour, then slowly floats to the ground for a landing.

All Fall Down

FREE FALL
The portion of the jump between exit from the plane and parachute deployment.

STATIC LINE JUMP
When a line attached to the aircraft is used to deploy the parachute. This kind of jump is used to train skydiving students or first-time jumpers.

TANDEM JUMP
A skydive during which two people use the same parachute system, each wearing a harness with one attached to the other. First-time jumpers like tandem jumps because they have an experienced diver strapped to them.

TERMINAL VELOCITY
The greatest speed at which something falls through Earth's atmosphere, or the velocity that a free falling body can attain against air resistance. Resistance of the air competing with the pull of gravity establishes the approximate figure of 150 to 176 feet (46 to 54 m) per second for the parallel-to-Earth position.

Activity

GOING TO EXTREMES Sports like skydiving are sometimes called "extreme" sports. That's because athletes who participate in this sport are in more danger of getting seriously hurt than athletes who participate in traditional sports. Research another extreme sport of your choice. You can choose from surfing, extreme snowboarding, bungee jumping, rock climbing, or any other extreme sport you'd like to learn more about. Use the Internet to read about this sport. What kinds of forces are at work? How do these forces and gravity affect the athlete's performance? Write a one-page report on your extreme sport, highlighting how the sport works and the dangers associated with it. Share your report with the class.

Balancing Act

SCRAPBOOK

SHORT STUFF

Professional football players are pretty hefty guys. Yet four of the top five all-time rushers, or ball carriers, are 5 feet 10 inches (1.8 m) in height or shorter: Walter Payton, Barry Sanders, Emmit Smith, and Tony Dorsett. These players are skilled athletes, but they've got something bigger players don't have: a lower center of gravity. Because they're shorter, their center of gravity is lower—making it difficult for larger players with higher centers of gravity to knock them off balance.

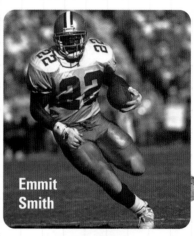

Emmit Smith

ook down at your belly button. Right about there is your body's center of gravity. The center of gravity is the point where all of gravity's effects are balanced—up, down, and sideways. The center of gravity varies for every object. In a skyscraper, a flagpole, or a tall tree, it's located about midway between the top and bottom and midway between the two sides.

FALLING OREOS

In 1998, ten-year-old Ross Tapley stacked up 23 Oreo™ Cookies in 30 seconds. He didn't want to dunk them in milk. He entered—and won—an Oreos Stacking Contest held by the Nabisco Company. Why only 23 sandwich cookies? The stack's center of gravity moved when the cookies were not placed directly on top of each other. As the stack shifted, the force of gravity pulling down on the cookies overcame the balancing forces. Almost two dozen cookies might seem like a mini-stack, but keep in mind that the contestants had just 30 seconds. One physicist calculated that, given unlimited time, a stack of more than 1000 Oreos could be built before collapsing. Give it a try. How many Oreos can you stack up before the column collapses? You'll have a tasty treat when you're done!

BEND YOUR KNEES!

Skiers, boarders, skaters, and surfers all get the same advice when they're starting out: bend your knees. How does that help? The first thing it does is to make your center of gravity lower, giving more power to the force connecting you with the surface of your skis, skates, or board. That means that the forces trying to knock you back, forward, or sideways have to work a lot harder. The second thing it does is make the fall shorter—which probably makes your body a whole lot happier.

16

Slugger Shift

Home run slugger Mark McGwire has lightning reflexes. But his center of gravity does a lot to send his home runs into the stands. Actually, it's the change of his center of gravity that helps him hit the homers. As he waits for a pitch, McGwire leans most of his 225-pound body weight on his back, or right, leg. That means his center of gravity is closer to his right hip than to his belly button. As this slugger swings his bat, he steps toward the ball with his left leg. That instantly shifts his center of gravity across his body toward the whizzing baseball. As the bat connects with the ball, McGwire's gravity-shifting body creates a powerful force that travels through the bat and into the ball, turning the pitch into a winning home run.

Gravity on Wheels

Why do bikers lean forward as they climb steep hills? The upward angle of the road changes the line of gravity from directly up and down to diagonal. To keep their cycles in balance, riders stretch their bodies forward over the handlebars, moving their centers of gravity up and forward—helping them pedal to the top of the hill.

What Comes Around . . .

Your center of gravity changes depending on your body's position, but the center of gravity in a human is always in the body. But when a boomerang is flying around in a circle, its center of gravity is not on the actual object. It's in the space between the two ends. When a boomerang is thrown, forces act to stop it from going straight. The thrown boomerang pushes through the air, and the boomerang lifts up as it is simultaneously pushed sideways by centripetal force. The combination of forces pushes it around in a circle.

Activity

GRAVITY A GO-GO Choose a favorite activity—anything except being a couch potato. Draw or write an explanation of how your center of gravity changes during the activity, the ways in which you can control it, and how being able to control it helps you.

Spook or Spoof?

There are places all over the world where the force of gravity seems to be suspended. Cars appear to roll uphill, and water looks like it's running upstream. What could be going on? Many of these unusual locations have become tourist attractions where guides might claim that there are strange—even ghostly— forces at work that science can't explain. This is not true. Science can describe what is happening. But the explanation has much more to do with human perception than an exemption from the law of gravity.

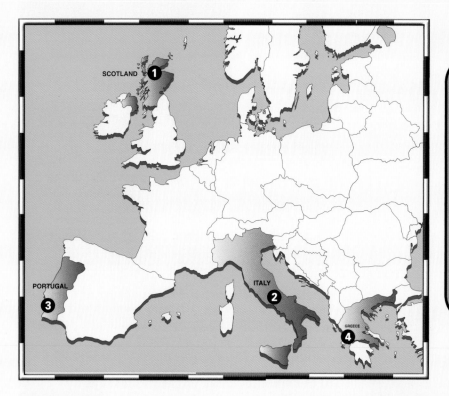

Psychology professors Arthur Shimamura and William Prinzmetal of the University of California at Berkeley studied "mystery spots" and presented a paper on these perceptual illusions at the annual meeting of the American Psychological Association in 1998. "Saying it's a visual illusion doesn't detract from the amazing experience of going there," Prinzmetal said. "It's still very strange."

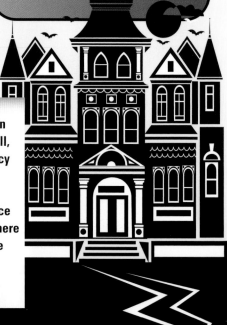

EUROPE

❶ Electric Brae, on A719 road near Croy Bay, Ayeshire, Scotland

❷ Hill South of Rome, in Colli Albani (White Hills), near Frascati, Italy

❸ Malveira da Serra, on N247 coast road, west of Lisbon, Portugal

❹ Mount Penteli, road leading to mountain, Athens, Greece

At each of the above sites, you can stop your car on the specified hill, cut the engine, release the emergency brake, and it LOOKS like your car is rolling uphill. But this is an optical illusion, created by nature. Each place is in a mountainous, coastal area where the horizon is partially obscured. The eye is fooled into thinking a slight downhill slope is actually uphill.

NATURAL

5 Gravity Hill, Salt Lake City, UT

6 Spook Hill, Lake Wales, FL

7 Oregon Vortex, Gold Hill, OR

8 Mystery Hill, Blowing Rock, NC

At each of these tourist attractions, there are natural phenomena that guides claim are gravitational oddities. Balls seem to roll uphill at Gravity Hill, Spook Hill and Mystery Hill. At the Oregon Vortex, compasses don't work, light is distorted, electricity is influenced, objects are pulled toward the center of the area, and paper scraps thrown up into the air tend to spiral as they fall.

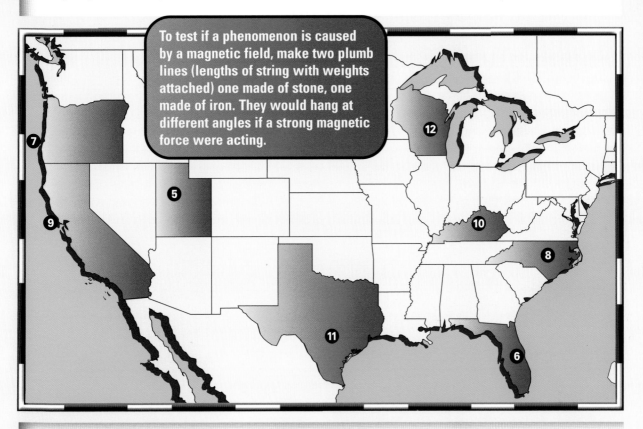

To test if a phenomenon is caused by a magnetic field, make two plumb lines (lengths of string with weights attached) one made of stone, one made of iron. They would hang at different angles if a strong magnetic force were acting.

HUMAN-MADE

9 Mystery Spot, Santa Cruz, CA

10 Big Mike's Mystery House, Cave City, KY

11 Wonder World, San Marcos, TX

12 Wonder Spot, Lake Delton, WI

These attractions are constructed by people who build odd houses where, they claim, gravity doesn't work. Brooms appear to stand on end, chairs balance off walls and visitors leave not knowing which way is up. Some guests even feel dizzy and nauseous. Guides may claim the illness is the effect of strange forces at work. A more likely explanation is that the balance mechanism in the inner ear has been disturbed by conflicting visual information. The bizarre illness is no more mysterious than motion sickness.

Activity

MYSTERY TOUR Do research on the Internet and use what you've learned about gravity to explain what is really going on at these and other "mystery spots." Try to find pictures of the phenomena, and explain what you see.

Black Hole:
Like No Place in Space

When it comes to science, have you ever felt dense? No matter how hard you try to understand some scientific concept, do you ever just give up and figure that your brain is too thick to get it? If you have, maybe you'd like to take a trip to a place in space that is denser than anywhere—or anyone—in the universe. That place is called a black hole.

Before we go, you might want to know just exactly where you're headed—in other words, what is a black hole? Black holes were once known as frozen stars, and, basically, that's what they are. Stars are gigantic furnaces. Because even smallish stars like the Sun are incredibly large, they have a powerful gravitational pull. That's why the planets in our Solar System orbit the Sun instead of careening madly through space like planetary pinballs.

A star's gravitational pull is balanced by a push outward from the energy at its core that keeps the fiery object from collapsing. When certain stars' energies die, or freeze, there may be no force left to push out from these stars' interiors. The pull force of gravity takes over and squeezes that star into a small, incredibly dense object. It's as if the largest mountain on Earth, Mount Everest, were compressed into an object the size of a marble—but with no loss of mass. That's dense with a capital D. From its center point, called the singularity, the black hole's pull is so powerful that nothing can move fast enough to escape its gravitational field—not even light. But instead of reading about them, let's go on a trip to the ultra-dense world of a black hole. We'll blast off from Earth in a rocket.

Ready?

Escaping from Earth's gravitational pull is a snap—all you have to do is reach a speed of about 25,000 miles per hour (40,225 km per hour). That's called escape velocity. Free of Earth's gravity, you head to the center of our galaxy, where astronomers believe that a black hole exists, one that is one million times heavier than our Sun. Because of the black hole's pull, you switch off your rockets far away from your destination and drift in. As you approach the dark circle in the distance, you witness a strange sight. There is a boundary: a curved band of light that is bent around the dark core. This is what astronomers call the event horizon. It is the farthest edge of the black hole's gravitational pull. The reason light stops at the boundary is that it cannot travel fast enough to escape from the gravitational grasp of the singularity. Strangely, as you approach the horizon, like any horizon, it seems to be still. Yet the light you see is still traveling at 186,000 miles (300,000 km) per second—and getting nowhere.

Oh, by the way, if any of your pals on Earth are watching, they'll lose sight of you once you cross the horizon. Any radio signals you send from the space ship can't escape from the black hole. So to those back home, you've disappeared.

Once across the event horizon, you feel the tidal pull of the hole's singularity, a pull similar to the power that moves oceans on Earth. Since your feet are closer to the hole than your head, you'll soon feel as though you're being stretched like a piece of taffy candy. Every atom in your body is being pulled apart.

Unfortunately, you're moving so fast now that there isn't much to see. Any objects outside the horizon are bent into strange shapes by the curved light that is held inside the gravity field of the black hole. Faster now, the time until you make contact with the singularity is just seconds away. You feel like toothpaste being squeezed out of a tube as the power of gravity pulls you apart. Remember what it feels like going down a big roller coaster drop? Your head seems to wait in the sky as your legs head toward Earth? This is like that coaster ride—times a zillion. Are you having fun yet? What's that? You want to go back home? You'd rather read about black holes than reach one? That could be a problem. You see, even though your spaceship had no problem reaching the 25,000 mile (40,225 km) per hour escape velocity from Earth, there's no way it can reach 186,000 miles (300,000 km) per second, the speed of light, to get out of the hole. In fact, your ship would have to go faster than that, since light can't even get away from the pull of a black hole. And faster than that is impossible. Perhaps it would have been wise to ask a little more about this trip before you climbed aboard.

You see, a voyage to a black hole is always a one-way trip.

Activity

FAR-OUT TRIP Let's say you've landed on the singularity of a black hole. Obviously, everything is compressed into tiny dense objects. If a mountain could become the size of a marble, how big are you? Once you get your bearings, you stop in at the Black Hole Dock and Dine. What do you have to eat? A heavy meal, no doubt. After the meal, you pick up some postcards. What's on the front? What message do you send back to Earth? Write a journal entry describing your visit to a dense—and imaginary—world.

Falling for Gravity

Between 1589 and 1592, the great scientist Galileo Galilei (1564–1642) taught geometry and astronomy at the University of Pisa in Italy. During those years, the young teacher also began writing a book he titled *On Motion.* That book was never published, but many of Galileo's ideas and experiments from that work, concerning gravity and falling bodies, were included in his later works.

Galileo lived more than a century before Sir Isaac Newton, the man who developed the laws of motion and gravity. Like Newton, Galileo had beliefs about the nature of the universe that were not accepted at the time. Throughout his life, Galileo made enemies of people in authority by questioning their scientific beliefs—beliefs handed down over the centuries and accepted without question. For Galileo, any truth had to be proved.

In this historical fiction, Galileo is pondering the relationship between falling bodies and gravity. The italicized words are direct quotes from Galileo.

Pisa, 1589: How foolish is the mob who blindly follows past teachings of ancients such as

Aristotle or Ptolemy! The study of our world must be done with one's own eyes. *In science, the opinion of thousands is not worth the thoughtful reasoning of a single individual.*

Pisa, 1590: I have long questioned Aristotle's teachings on the motion of falling bodies. Most accept his statement that the speed of a falling body remains the same throughout the fall. This troubles me. Even more troubling is the acceptance of his teaching that the weight of a falling body determines the speed of its fall.

Following that line of reason, let us suppose that two objects—one with a weight of 22 pounds (10 kilograms), the other 11 pounds (5 kg)—were dropped from the same height. According to Aristotle, the heavier object would reach Earth twice as fast as the lighter object. Though it might seem logical—and indeed it has been accepted for generations—I cannot accept Aristotle's teaching without experiment. For me, a truth cannot be reached unless *we measure what is measurable and make measurable what is not.*

Were it possible, I would present the esteemed Greek with the following hypothesis: Suppose I were to ascend to the top of the

tower here in Pisa with the two objects I previously described. Now suppose I were to connect the two with a string and drop the new joined object. By attaching the lighter, slower-falling weight, would I in fact slow the fall of the new object? Or would the linking of the two make the new object—now 33 pounds (15 kg) in total—fall one and one-half times faster than the 22-pound (10-kg) object and three times faster than the 11-pound (5-kg) object? For Aristotle's teaching to hold true, the answer to both questions would have to be yes. Yet common sense tells us that the answer to both questions is no. This division between unthinking belief and thoughtful reason is but one example of the failure of our society today. *For who can deny that the worst disorders occur when we are told to deny our senses and submit to an outside will?*

Pisa, 1591: My mind has been consumed with proving my theories of falling bodies. In direct disagreement with Aristotle, I contend that when two objects of differing weights are dropped, the lighter object will move ahead of the heavier body in the initial moments of the fall. Next, it is my claim that the speed of a falling object increases over the time of its fall. Further, I contend that all objects fall at the same speed, regardless of their weight, drawn downward by the force of the ground beneath our feet.

Pisa, 1592: Many hours of work and thought have helped to redirect my hypotheses of falling bodies. My students have assisted in performing, observing, and measuring my experiments. From Pisa's leaning tower, we repeatedly dropped two spheres of identical size, one of wood and one of iron. We observed that indeed the wooden spheres moved ahead of the iron as the fall began.

As to the other aspects of my theory, the iron object did indeed strike ground before the wooden sphere. However, the iron sphere had a weight ten times

greater than that of wood. Observers agreed that the heavier object did not fall at a rate ten times greater than the lighter object. Though my theory that all objects fall at the same speed was not proved, that of Aristotle was disproved. Finally, my third contention involving the increase of speed over the time of a fall was one that resisted mathematical measurement and thus remains unproved. Though I have no doubt of its truth, *the laws of the universe cannot be read until they are written in mathematical language, without which they are impossible to comprehend.*

Florence, 1636: As I complete my latest work, *Two New Sciences*, I am at last able to advance my theory of falling bodies: In a setting without the resistance of air, all bodies fall at the same speed and gain equal amounts of speed during the time of the fall.

Activity

SPEED CONTROL After his experiments at Pisa, Galileo realized that the resistance of air made it impossible to prove his theory that all objects fall at the same rate of speed. Now that we have traveled into the airless and weightless environment of space, his theory has been tested. What variables must be controlled when testing gravity's effect on the rate of speed of different objects? Design an experiment that controls these variables and could be implemented on the Moon.

MAJOR MOVES

A Well Balanced
PISA

The Leaning Tower of Pisa was accidently built on unstable soil in 1173. After just three floors were built, the tower started sinking, adding about one-twentieth of an inch to its tilt per year. It now leans almost 14.5 feet (4.5 m) away from vertical. In 1990, engineers feared that the famous building might tumble and closed it to stabilize the foundation. Why did it take so long for the people of Pisa to take action? Until then, the Tower was balanced. One consideration for this lies in the placement of the building's center of gravity.

Basically, an object's center of gravity is the point at which gravity is focused on the object. If this point changes, the object may tip over. An easy way to understand this is to think about your own center of gravity, which lies near your belly button. If you draw a line straight down from your center of gravity to the ground, it will fall somewhere between your feet. You are able to bend or lean without falling over just as long as that line stays between your feet. If you lean too far you'll topple.

The same principle can be applied to the Leaning Tower of Pisa. If you draw a line from its center of gravity to the ground, you'll find that the line still touches the base of the building. Although the Tower's center of gravity is getting about as close as it can to the edge of the base, it still hasn't reached it. So, until the building's foundation sinks deeply enough into the ground for its center of gravity to exceed the edge of its base, the Leaning Tower will stand. After all, you can lean pretty far over before you fall.

Jiving with Java

What do you have in common with a spill-proof coffee cup when you're standing on a moving train? Quite a lot. The first thing that you probably do when you get on a train is spread out your feet. This makes it harder for you to fall over if the train jerks because you have more room to lean from side to side. The same principle holds with spill-proof coffee cups. The base is much wider than a normal coffee cup—which means that you'd have to knock it pretty hard to tip it.

The Spin on Basketballs and Bicycles

Seeing someone spin a basketball on their index finger is amazing. Need proof? Try to balance a ball on the tip of your finger. It's tough to do—unless you spin it! The spinning motion stabilizes the ball by establishing what is called angular momentum.

Spinning also constantly redistributes the center of gravity. Instead of falling down, the ball sticks around its balancing point—your finger. The faster you spin the ball, the more easily it "sticks" to your finger. When the ball begins to slow down, the angular momentum still holds it on your finger. As it slows more, it starts spinning off balance.

Though you'll probably never slam dunk a basketball while riding a mountain bike, riding a bicycle and spinning a basketball on your finger have a lot in common. Both gain stability from a spinning motion. The center of gravity plays some role in bike riding, but most of the credit lies in the angular momentum created by the bikes' two spinning wheels, which help to keep it upright. Just as in the basketball example, the faster you spin the wheels on the bike, the greater the momentum and the more stable the ride is. It's actually much harder to stay balanced at slower speeds because the force isn't as strong. And when a bike isn't moving, it's impossible for it to stay balanced or stand alone—that's why bikes have kickstands.

Activity

LIVE A BALANCED LIFE Carmakers have recently started taking center of gravity into consideration much more. That's why they're building wider, more stable cars. Look around your school and find things that you would redesign to make them less likely to tip over. Draw a picture of your new design and share it with your class.

25

Mission Mix-Up

A group of five kids was chosen to go on a top secret Solar System mission. Their assignment: Gather information and conduct experiments on every planet except Earth. The kids were broken up into various groups: Some were assigned partners, others flew solo, and some teamed up with more than one group during different points in the mission. The problem? All their information and data got mixed up. The only accurate information NASA has is each astronaut's weight on every planet. The only way to decipher the data is to figure out who visited what planet and with whom. Can you figure it out? Use the gravity factors listed on page 13 to calculate the kid astronauts' weights. Round decimals .5 and above up to the nearest whole number and .4 and below down to the nearest whole number. Then use the clues to solve this mission mix-up. Make a chart to help you keep track of the missions.

Mission Groups

Mission One:
- One female and one male partnered up to visit three planets.

Mission Two:
- Another female and another male partnered up to visit three other planets.

Mission Three:
- Two people visited Venus together.

Mission Four:
- Three people visited Jupiter together.

Weight of each astronaut on Earth

Christopher	101 pounds
Keisha	82 pounds
Janice	97 pounds
Carla	82 pounds
Thomas	138 pounds

QUESTIONS:

1. Who visited Venus?
2. Which planets did Keisha visit?
3. Which planets did Janice visit? Who was her partner?
4. How many planets did Christopher visit?
5. Who had the most partners throughout the entire mission?
6. Which three visited one planet together?
7. Where did Carla go? With whom?
8. Look at the group scenarios and clues. Put everyone in the right groups.

clueS

Use these clues . . .

1. The weight of the two who went to Mars was 31 pounds and 52 pounds. These two had a combined weight of 204 pounds on another planet. They also visited one more planet, where one of them weighed 3 pounds.

2. The two who visited Venus had a combined weight of 217 pounds while there.

3. One female weighed 77 and 109 pounds on Uranus and Neptune, respectively. With her partner, their combined weight on one planet was 223 pounds.

4. The combined weight of the three who visited one planet together was 707 pounds.

5. Carla did not visit Pluto.

Answers on page 32.

The Apple of My Eye

Isaac Newton (1642–1727)

More than being the "apple guy," Isaac Newton is one of the greatest mathematicians and physicists of all time. Born on December 25, 1642, Newton spent his life experimenting with and challenging scientific ideas. His famous law says that gravity is a force that occurs between two things, and this force is affected by the size of the objects and how far apart they are.

In his book, *Memoirs of Sir Isaac Newton's Life*, William Stukeley explains a conversation he had with Newton about the theory of gravity:

"After dinner, the weather being warm, we went into the garden and drank tea, under shade of some apple-trees, only he and myself. Amidst other discourses, he told me, he was just in the same situation, as when formerly, the notion of gravitation came into his mind. It was occasion'd by the fall of an apple, as he sat in contemplative mood. Why should that apple always descend perpendicularly to the ground, thought he to himself. Why should it not go sideways or upwards, but constantly to the earth's center? Assuredly, the reason is, that the earth draws it. There must be a drawing power in matter: and the sum of the drawing power in the matter of the earth must be in the earth's center, not in any side of the earth."

Newton believed, correctly, that because Earth is so much bigger than everything on it, its gravitational pull is the strongest. That's why we're all pulled to Earth's center and don't fall off into space.

Gravitational Goodies

Without Newton, we might not have the knowledge of gravity that we have today—or a lot of fun and useful things. Check out this stuff to see how gravity works around you.

Radical Roller Coasters

Roller coasters rely on gravity to go. Gravity pulls the cars down a hill, and the momentum the cars gather as they go down propels them up the next hill. And check out one of those looping roller coasters! Once you're strapped in and get to the top of the loop, gravity pulls you toward the ground, but momentum pushes you forward. Gravity slows you down as you reach the top, then accelerates you as you start to descend the loop.

What Goes Up...

A skier competes at Blackcomb Mountain, British Columbia, Canada. The speed he gathers as he skis down the ramp launches this competitor skyward. But as he performs flips and twists, he races against gravity, which continues to pull him down.

Zero Gravity at Zero Gravity

People of all ages defy gravity at Zero Gravity Skate Park located in Rutland, Vermont. Momentum takes skaters and bikers up the steep ramp, but gravity eventually pulls them back down.

Space Case

As they watch astronauts twisting and flipping inside the space shuttle, most people think they're floating. Actually, the sensation is more like a free fall, but because of their surroundings, astronauts are able to avoid feeling like they are falling. R. Mike Mullane, an astronaut on three space shuttle missions, says: "No doubt about it, weightlessness can be fun, excluding the vomiting and backache. With just a touch of a finger you can send your body flying across the cockpit, and heavy items that we struggle to deal with in Earth simulations can be effortlessly moved."

Activity

BALL FALL You'll need two balls, one heavier than the other. You'll also need a smooth piece of cardboard and some clay. First, drop the balls from the same height at the same time onto the cardboard. Which one hit first? Next, roll the clay over the cardboard, making sure it's smooth. Drop the balls onto the clay-covered surface. Which one hit first? Which one sank deeper into the clay? Why? Write a paragraph explaining your thoughts.

GRAVITY: The Picker Upper

Need a Lift?

Have you ever seen someone magically lifted into the air? That trick was first performed by a magician named Balducci. The Balducci Levitation is an illusion that has tricked audiences into believing that someone or something can float in the air. Usually, there is some kind of string that brings the person into the air. That's why it's an illusion—it doesn't happen for real.

But physicists have been experimenting with levitation for years. In 1996, European scientists made headlines with an experiment that levitated a live frog. How did they do it? All materials, including humans, are slightly magnetic. If the materials are in a really strong magnetic field, the atoms they are made of can change motion and make an opposite magnetic field. If the magnetic field is vertical, the magnetic force can overcome gravity and cause the object to levitate. But don't try this at home! The magnetic forces are so strong they can become dangerous to living things. Scientists used an intense electromagnetic field to make the frog float. And, to date, they still haven't succeeded in creating an electromagnetic field strong enough to levitate a person. So it's probably a good idea to keep your feet on the ground.

TALL TALE

Without gravity, your spine would extend—and make you taller. That's what happens to astronauts in space: They stretch by about 2 inches (5 cm). But you don't have to visit Mars to see how gravity affects your height. Try this experiment to see what happens to your height when gravity kicks in.

1. Tape a blank piece of paper at eye level to a door.

2. As soon as you wake up in the morning, grab a ruler and pencil and head to that door. Stand barefoot with your back against the door. Lay the ruler flat on top of your head and use the pencil to mark the spot where the ruler hits the paper. You can ask someone for help if you need it.

3. Before you go to bed that night, measure yourself like you did that morning. Where is the second mark? Why?

4. Measure yourself again the next morning. What happened? Why do you think that happens?

FACE LiFt

On Earth, your body and gravity are always fighting. Gravity wants to yank your organs, muscles, and bones down, but your body wants to keep them up. Luckily, on Earth, the battle ends in a tie. But in space, gravity loses, hands down (or hands up!). When gravity's effects are lessened, your body goes haywire. Everything goes up. Water and blood rush to your head—that makes your face swell and your legs get skinnier. What would your face look like in space? Hang your head upside down and look into a mirror. Can you see what's happening? Fluids rush down into your face and gravity drags your face towards the ground. In space, fluids distribute themselves equally throughout your body, and there's not enough gravity to pull your face down.

Moon Zoom

Why doesn't the Moon fly into outer space? Thank gravity. Its force holds the Moon as it revolves around Earth. How does it work? Try this at home to figure it out.

1 Take a tennis ball and wrap an elastic band around it a few times.

2 Attach a 2-foot-long (.6-m-long) string to the elastic band on the ball. Make sure it's secure.

3 Clear everything—and everyone—out of your way. Grab the string at the other end and swing it quickly around your head for a minute.

4 What happens? The ball gets lifted up and travels in a horizontal circle around your head. The spinning action and the string acts as gravity, holding the ball in a steady circle. But if you let go of the string—and cut off the gravity—the ball will go flying. Luckily, Earth's gravitational pull doesn't let go. If it did, the Moon would go flying off into space.

His Airness

If there's one athlete that defies gravity, it's Michael Jordan, called by many the best athlete of the twentieth century. Dubbed "His Airness," this famous former Chicago Bulls basketball star seemed to float in the air each time he jumped up to make a basket. When Jordan jumped up for a shot, it looked like he'd hover in the air forever. Jordan never actually defied gravity with his high leaps and broad jumps—he just tried to challenge Newton's laws. It's even true for Michael Jordan: what goes up, must come down.

Motion Potion

Without gravity, your sense of balance goes bonkers. Your inner ears contain tiny motion sensors. In zero gravity, those sensors send confusing signals to your brain because they can't tell which way is up. At the same time, your eyes see that the floor is down and the ceiling is up. These confusing signals between your eyes and ears make you sick—really. That's why some people get motion sickness. People get sick after a twisty, upside-down roller coaster ride because their signals and, ultimately, their hormones get messed up. Astronauts go through the same thing as they float around in space. How can you try not getting nauseous over less gravity? Keep your eyes closed so they don't mix up your ear sensors, and move slowly without shaking your head. That usually helps astronauts settle their zero gravity gags.

YOUR WORLD YOUR TURN

Deep End of the Ocean

Imagine a world with nothing holding you back—or down. In the 1960s, oceanographer Jacques Yves Cousteau tried to make that dream a reality. Cousteau was determined to prove humans could live underwater. So he started a project called Conshelf. It was at Conshelf that living underwater—without Earth's restrictive forces—became a reality.

In 1962, Cousteau's Conshelf allowed two scientists to live 85 feet (26 m) below the sea for one week. While part of the Conshelf mission was to explore the mysteries of the deep, the "oceanauts" were determined to show that humans can and should live beneath the sea. With that project a success, Cousteau continued his work with Conshelf II. He and five scientists lived 36 feet (11 m) below the surface of the Red Sea for one month. But deep-sea living caused some deep problems. Limited air supply, decompression dangers, and low underwater visibility was tough on the oceanauts. And living in tight quarters for one month—without a land escape—was no holiday. Cousteau's underwater living experiment at Conshelf II was turned into an Academy Award winning movie, *World Without Sun*.

Because of Cousteau's pioneering underwater journey, other scientists and government agencies built underwater human habitats, too. From 1964 to 1969, five different aquatic living habitats were built for experiments. Today, several aquatic human "homes" are used for science—and tourism. The reason? To explore the underwater world—and to show that living underwater is feasible should Earth become too polluted to support human life.

Do some research to learn about other marine human habitats that were set up. What kind of obstacles did the oceanauts face as they tried to set up shop underwater? What forces and pressures affected Cousteau and other ocean explorers in their quest for an underwater home?

Taking into consideration everything you know about water buoyancy, gravity, and other pressures, build an underwater habitat for you and your family. Draw a picture and explain how your underwater home would work. What would it look like? How would your home—and your family—safely stay underwater? What kinds of things would be necessary in your water home to help you lead a life similar to people still living on land?

"Man has only to sink beneath the surface and he is free. Buoyed by water, he can fly."
—Jacques Yves Cousteau

ANSWERS Solve-It-Yourself Mystery, pages 26–27

1. Chris and Thomas
2. Mars, Saturn, Pluto, and Jupiter
3. Uranus, Neptune, Mercury; Christopher was Janice's partner
4. Four: Uranus, Neptune, Mercury, and Venus
5. Thomas, Keisha, Christopher, and Carla
6. Carla, Keisha, and Thomas
7. Carla went to Jupiter with Keisha and Thomas
8. Mission Groups:

Mission One:
Keisha and Thomas went to Mars, Saturn, and Pluto

Mission Two:
Janice and Christopher went to Uranus, Neptune, and Mercury

Mission Three:
Chris and Thomas visited Venus together

Mission Four:
Thomas, Keisha, and Carla went to Jupiter